Echoes
from the
Depths
of Hale

Samuel W. Hale, Jr.

WESTBOW
PRESS®
A DIVISION OF THOMAS NELSON
& ZONDERVAN

WestBow Press books may be ordered through booksellers or by contacting:

WestBow Press
A Division of Thomas Nelson & Zondervan
1663 Liberty Drive
Bloomington, IN 47403
www.westbowpress.com
844-714-3454

All Scripture quotations are taken from the King James Version, public domain.

ISBN: 979-8-3850-1755-3 (sc)
ISBN: 979-8-3850-1756-0 (e)

Library of Congress Control Number: 2024901446

Print information available on the last page.

WestBow Press rev. date: 01/29/2024

Contents

ME TO GOD

ME TO ME

ONE ON ONE

BREAKING OF THE CHAINS

AFFIRMATIONS - HALE-VERBS

MAN AND WOMAN

A LOOK AT LOVE

COMPLEMENTATION

IN LIFE – IN DEATH

MELODICA

Enlightenment

---⌢---

I heard Terah the Elder pray.
His words touched the inner essence of my soul.

I approached the old man and said,
"Yesterday I worshipped with feeling.
Today I shall worship with meaning!"

The old man spoke unremoved -
"Shall your meaningful worship be void of feeling?"

And Terah walked away.

Samuel W. Hale, Jr.

⌢

Introduction

Four-score plus one years, and counting,…
Have been my Conscious Days.
And through those years these words have come
To lament, assess, and praise.

So, as You read - even contemplate -
These words I share with You,
May they stimulate Your Heart and Mind,
Revealing Your Life Expressions too.

Take time to think and contemplate
Life's experiences - both Old and New -
Then comprehend and understand
What God has brought You through.

E ven in my childhood I found myself thinking and trying to
fathom the many things that I was experiencing in Life. People,
words, actions, interactions, nature, the seen, the unseen,
the known, the unknown, the feelings, the emotions, the cares, the
unconcerns that flood our daily experiences and encounters.

It wasn't long before I found myself following the example of my second-grade friend, **"Flukie"**! On wide-lined dotted paper, with fat one flat-sided pencils, we began to write our feelings, our thoughts, and our childhood words of "wisdom".

Throughout these many years that followed, that penchant to graphically preserve those thoughts, feelings, observations, and conclusions has grown, and has somewhat been enhanced and improved. And without shame, I dare reveal many of those evolutionary contemplations.

Most of these scribal introspections and declarations occurred from my early high school days through the present, as I approach my 82nd birthday. They include some poems, speeches, simple "musings", even some reflections following the Home Going of my former Wife of Fifty years! Each expression **echoing** from deep within me.

Thus, the title:
"Echoes from the Depths of Hale"

Read! Reflect!
And Listen Deeply with the Ears of Your Mind and Heart!

ME TO GOD

The Lord Has Need of Preachers

———— ∾ ————

The Lord has need of Preachers to heed the Spirit's Call
  To tell the dying sinner that Jesus died for all;
That God is standing ready to lift the stain of Sin,
  If he would just surrender and let the Savior in.

The Lord has need of Preachers to stand upon the Wall,
  And there proclaim the Message that Jesus died for All!
And when someone accepts Him as Savior of his soul,
  He'll have the Lord's Assurance to reach the Heavenly Goal.

The Lord has need of Preachers who stray not from the Word
  That saves the dying sinner who believes what he has heard
About the Blood of Jesus, Who died upon the Cross,
  And the freeness of Salvation for every Soul that's lost.

The Lord has need of Preachers who are not afraid to die
  By the hands and tongues of men who would rather live a lie.
But who would await the Coming Savior Who comes in Cloven Skies
  To take him Home to Glory, who lives and never dies.

The Lord has need of Preachers who live the Gospel well;
      Who have no fear of Satan, his demons, nor of Hell;
Who preach the Gospel Message with Faith and Fear of God;
      And who without reluctance will tread the Road Christ trod.

Lord, help Me be the Preacher that You would have Me be;
      And help Me tell the Story that sets the Sinner free.
Help Me to Preach the Gospel, in season and without,
      That Souls may turn to Jesus to praise Him with a Shout!

Lord, help Me be the Preacher that this World truly needs,
      And guide Me as I study the Gospel Word that feeds
The hungry, starving Sinner who lies in pain, near dead,
      Whose spirit seeks reviving from Christ, the Living Bread.

Lord, help Me be the Preacher on whom You can rely
      To spread the Gospel Story that helps men not to die.
Help Me to reach the children, whose tender souls receive
      The Saving Love of Jesus the hour they first believe.

Lord, help Me be the Preacher whose only Goal today
      Is to stand in Final Judgment and hear You kindly say,
"Come up, My stalwart Preacher, My Word you did declare.
      Behold this Crown of Glory, I give for You to wear!"

Samuel W. Hale, Jr. – 1997

The Reluctant Disciple

There is a certain Young Disciple
Whom the Lord has Called to Serve –
To reach the special group of Souls
Who get on each other's nerve.

That special group of Folks
Who dwell on the Other Side of the Street –
The Ones Enshackled by the Hedges of this World.
The Ones facing Obstacles that they alone can't beat.

That special group of People –
Circumscribed by Forces they can't control.
Circumstances and Situations, each Intended
And Designed to Demoralize the Soul.

Now that certain Young Disciple –
Seeing things that Church Folk cared not to hide –
Had some issues with what He saw and faced,
So He retreated to that Other Side.

And when He found himself entrenched
Within the Concerns of a different Life.
Some he mastered. With some he struggled.
And those Lifestyles soon brought Him strife.

But the issues of Guilt, Regret, and Shame
Need not linger on Life's Shelf.
For each and all can be Redeemed
When the Soul comes to Itself!

One day that Reluctant Disciple
Faced a moment that He could not easily tune out –
For the cries of His Friends and Neighbors
Touched his Heart with a mournful shout!

They had turned to Him for Answers.
They looked to Him for Comfort too.
They seemed to know that He offered Something
That could give them Hope anew.

Reluctant though He seemed to feel inside,
He could not seem to help Himself.
Whatever they seemed to seek from Him,
He had placed on Avoidance's Shelf!

But the Reassuring Voice of Jesus said,
"My Son, I have a Special Task for You.
I've Led and Kept You here On This Other Side,
For a Special Work designed for You to do.

Reluctant though You may have become;
Offended though You may even feel,
I chose Your Voice to Speak to Them.
Like Yours, Their Hurt is also Real.

You are still My Chosen Disciple,
Though is seems You may not want to be.
But I have Chosen and I have Nurtured You
To bring Redemption to those who would Follow Thee.

Within these Hedges and along Life's Highways
I have made You feel a part.
For now You Better can Understand
What still harbors in their Hearts.

Who better yet to Heal the Wounded?
Who better yet to Lead the Lost,
Than One who has Himself experienced
The Price that Lostness Costs!

Come now, My Reluctant Disciple!

'Tis time to compel those on the Other Side –
Tell Those who Hopeless and Helpless be
That a Feast awaits for them to share –
And a New Life for Them ALL to see!

Tell Them that God alone for Them provides
What seems They could not receive.
For the things they need to succeed in Life
Come through God, when they patiently Believe!

And while You Tell them, why don't You Show them
What their Faith in God will do;
For then it's easier to persuade those others
When they see God's Grace revealed through You!

God alone has all the Answers
For those things Men seek for Wealth.
Those things that Men often cling to –
Though they don't belong on Eternity's Shelf.

Come now, Thou Reluctant Disciple!
God calls You from Your "retreative" Place.
Lead those Seekers from the "Other Side"
Unto God, Who still includes Them in His Plan of Grace!

Know that Reluctance is a Hope that needs Assurance.
Know that Reluctance is a Hurt needing to be Healed.
And that One's Discipleship will be Redemptive
When Ones Calling is not Concealed!

A Prayer for Help

Lord, Grant Me the Faith to Believe that I Can…
The Satisfaction in Knowing that I Did…
The Conviction that I can Do It Again…
The Assurance that It will be Done…
And the Wisdom to Know that You Helped Me Do It!
And Lord, Help Me to Help Others Do the Same.

At Home Alone With God

I awaken to Life's circumstances
That are not designed for my control.
I confront some situations
That, alone, mine hands can't hold.

There are things that seem impossible.
There are solutions that take some time.
There are Answers that are Hidden.
There are answers - not worth a dime.

I may sail the whole World over.
I may climb to the mountain peak.
Even wade through four-leafed fields of clover
For the answers that I seek.

Though I counsel with Men of Wisdom -
To the thoughts of Fools I may give a nod.
But the Answers to Life's great Problems
Reside within the Omniscient Mind of God.

So I search for Life's hidden Answers –
Down mental paths I trod.
But I find the right solutions when
I seek and follow the Word of God.

Fruitlessly, I've tested my own Mind's Conjectures.
Even down Forbidden Paths I've trod.
But the Place and Time for Life's Deeper Revelations
Is when I'm at Home Alone with God.

God's Love and Me

It is God's Love that changes Me
From the Me I Am to the Me I am to Be!

It is God's Love that makes Me Flee
From the people and places I don't need to See!

It is God's Love instilled in Me
That makes Me Love those who are not like Me.

It is God's Love that sets Me Free
From the grip that Sin would hold on Me.

It is God's Love that makes Me See
That all things aren't as they ought to Be!

It is God's Love that causes Me
To want for Myself what God wants for Me.

It is God's Love most assuredly
That allowed Christ's Blood to be shed for Me.

It is God's Love that heartens Me
That some Day soon His Face I'll see!

Oh, may You come, my Friend, to see
That the Love of God is also there for Thee!

ME TO ME

Ah, Life...

Imperfect People
Raising Imperfect Children
In an Imperfect World
That Resists a Perfect God,
In Whom is the Perfect Life...

I Am That I Am

My Nature Cannot be Changed,
Nor Be My Spirit Broken
By any Derogatory Name Ascribed to Me,
When Written, Thought, or even Spoken!

Aging...

———————— ∽ ————————

Ah, Aging!
That Process where What Was
Begins to Morph into What Isn't...
And that Which Wasn't
Subtly Merges into What Is...
Yet, in the Midst of the Morphing and the Merging
Is still Revealed the Me that I Am!

∽

Assurance

The Day has come -
The die is cast.
I rise in Faith to transcend at last
The Assignment which has been my Task.

I view the Way I am to go;
The Future clear I do not know.
I venture forth - assured I can -
I've placed my Soul in God's Keeping Hands.

Reassurance

When Reason cries, "The Road is Dark!"
When Sight confess' it cannot see;
Then without haste, Old Faith replies,
"I know the Way, just Follow Me!"

When the Road gets Hard and Strength doth Fail;
When I Drift out on Life's Fitful Sea;
Then Faith Extends a Welcomed Hand,
And bids, "Sail on! Sail on with Me!"

Divine Assurances

When I lay me down in Death to sleep.
I know the Lord my Soul will keep.
I shall awake with a Crownly Diadem,
And with a Countenance Fair –
Looking just like Him!

"Beloved, now are we the sons of God,
and it doth not yet appear what we shall be:
but we know that, when he shall appear,
we shall be like him;
for we shall see him as he is."
- 1 John 3:2 (KJV)

Introspection

I searched the interior of My Soul to find the "Me's" that in Me Be.
I found the Me I Think I am, and the Me I Want to Be.
I found the Me I want You to See, and the Me God Created Me to Be.

I tried to comprehend each Me I found, to see the "most" of Me.
And interestingly I came to find, that of all the "Me's" I Be,
That the lesser of all the "Me's" I Be is the Me God Created Me to Be.

The Inner Struggle

The Struggles Between the Spirit and the Flesh
are Waged on the Battlefield of the Mind.
And the Winners of Each Battle are then
Revealed by the Actions of the Body…

A Living Tragedy

Oh, the Blessings of God's Forgiveness
That may Linger on Life's Shelf -
To Forgive the Mistakes of Others,
But to Fail to Forgive Oneself.

 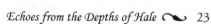

Incomparable

The Expansiveness and Pervasiveness
of the Love of God Transcends by Far
the Self-centeredness and Self-limitingness of Man.

Progress

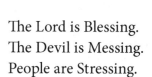

The Lord is Blessing.
The Devil is Messing.
People are Stressing.
But I'm Still Pressing!

Determined Progress...

That Fortitude to press forward with all of the deliberate speed
of a pregnant turtle crawling uphill in a snowstorm...

Victory

My Body says, "I Want!"
My Mind cautions, "Don't!"
My Spirit says, "I Won't!"

My Body says, "Now!"
My Mind cautions, "Not Yet!"
My Spirit says, "Not at All!"

My Body says, "Me First!"
My Mind Echoes, "Why Not Now?"
My Spirit says, "Be Patient!"

Oh, Where, When, Shall I Find Victory?

 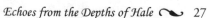

Life's Continuous
Balancing Act

To **Get** what You **Want**, and to **Want** what You **Get**.
To **Get** what You **Need**, and to **Need** what You **Get**.

To **Want** what You **Need**, and to **Need** what You **Want**.
To **Want** what You **Have**, and to **Have** what You **Need**.

To **Have** what You **Want**, and to **Want** what You **Get**.
To **Have** what You **Need**, and to **Need** what You **Have**.

My Parental Affirmation

I Believed In and was Committed To the Lord Jesus Christ Before I
    Became a Man.
I Became a Servant of God Before I Became a Preacher of the Gospel.
I Became a Preacher of the Gospel before I Became a Husband.
I Became a Pastor – a Shepherd - before I Became a Father, and a
    Grandparent.
I cannot Cease Being Me without Being Either.

I cannot Be Husband, Father, and a Grandparent
Without Being a Shepherd and Teacher to My Family.
In order to Be a Shepherd and Teacher to My Family,
I must Proclaim and Lead Them to a Saving Relationship with God.
Then I can Best Help Them to Be and to Become All that God Created
    Them to Be.

Each – My Wife, My Children, My Grandchildren (and Theirs too) –
Must Strive for Themselves to Establish Their Chosen Relationship
    with God.
However They Choose to Relate to God will Directly Affect how They
    Relate to Me.
Yet, I can Only Be as Much of a Husband, Father, and Grandparent
As Either will Let Me Be to Them.

Still, I Must Continue to Be the Soul that God Leads Me to Be -
Whether Preacher, Pastor, Teacher, Husband, Father, and
    Grandfather -
However I might Be Accepted by Those who Choose to Relate to Me,
The Choice and Effort is Theirs, and shall Forever Be.
And so the Same shall Be to Those to Whom They shall Strive to Be!

Sometimes I'm Called to be Preacher, Pastor, Teacher, Husband,
    Father, Grandfather, and Great-grandfather.
Yet I Understand that However I am Seen and Called and Needed,
Whomever and Whatever may Be Desired or Expected of Me,
I still can only be to that Person as much of what they Allow Me to
    Be to Them!
…And So Will You Be to those with whom You encounter!

Understanding

⸺⸺ ⸎ ⸺⸺

Understanding is the Ability To See…
Above the Horizon,
Beneath the Surface,
And Beyond the Obvious…

Understanding allows One to…
Connect the Proper Dots…
Envision the Unseen…
And Comprehend the Unrevealed…

Understanding allows One to…
Expect the Unexpected…
Overcome the Unanticipated…
And Recognize the Impossible…

Understanding allows One to…
Explore the Unexplored…
Avoid the Destructible…
And Conquer the Unconquered…

Understanding allows One to...
Pray for what is Promised...
Weigh the Improbable...
And Await the Assured...

Understanding allows One to...
Relate to the Unrelated...
Discern the Uncomprehended...
And Explain the Unexplained...

Understanding allows One to...
Recognize One's Limitations...
Strive to Fulfill One's Potential...
And Maximize One's Opportunities...

Understanding allows One to...
Appreciate the Accomplished...
Anticipate the Possible...
And Expect the Eternal...

"...and with all thy getting get understanding."
- Proverbs 4:7 (KJV)

Life's Transitions

It's hard to say it, Truth be told,
But I must admit, I'm getting old.
And because the shape my body's in,
I must rely on my "depends".

It "depends" on how I'm feeling
When I wake up every morn -
Whether I will get up out of bed,
Or just fall back to sleep, like a baby newly born.

It "depends" on whether my prescriptions
Need refilling - or maybe – just need be changed.
It "depends" on if my hearing aid is fully charged,
Or maybe just out of range.

It "depends" on if it's raining,
Or if I'm only getting chilled.
It "depends" if it's just my co-pay,
Or if I'm actually getting billed.

It "depends" if my dentures stay in place
Whene'er I start to smile.
Or if I used enough deodorant -
Be it lately, or for quite a while.

It "depends" on if my Social Security check
Will be delivered just in time;
Or need I sign away this month's Pension -
There on the dotted line.

Be it aging, or just incontinence,
Or whatever Life yet sends.
However You choose to go through Life,
I'll still rely on my "depends".

ONE ON ONE

Jump Start!

When I perceive how God has Touched Me,
I am reminded Day and Night –
And I'm Challenged by His Holy Spirit
With THIS Divine Directive – **"Write"**!

The True Message

Speak Thou Gently from Thine Heart…
Give Ignorance nor Anger a Place to Start.
For What You Say and How You Say it
Impacts the Hearer as You Convey It.

Pass It On

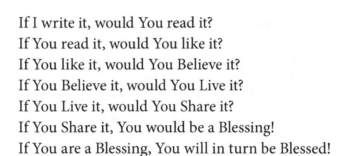

If I write it, would You read it?
If You read it, would You like it?
If You like it, would You Believe it?
If You Believe it, would You Live it?
If You Live it, would You Share it?
If You Share it, You would be a Blessing!
If You are a Blessing, You will in turn be Blessed!

Just Be True

Tempt me not with words untrue,
Nor coax with smiles forlorn;
For lies are told by crooks, my dear,
And that, you were not born.

Poetic Justice

When I invited You to join my Presence,
You chose instead that place to Spit!
How ironic! Where You expressed Indifference,
Was the only place left to Sit.

Friends

Stand Thou with Me, and I with Thee,
In facing Friends, and Foes, and Family.
Then, when Life gets Hard for Me and Thee,
We know that God will Our Deliverer Be!

* * *

Good, Gooder, Goodest

'Tis said that Blood is thicker than Water -
A Bond that binds, as Bonding should.
But to shed one's Blood to Save Another
'Tis to Serve the Greater Good!

John 15:9

God has made You His Special Vessel
Into which He imparts His Special Love,
And He gives You Divine Potential
To Share with Others His Love from Up Above.

So I do not ask for You to Love Me -
I Believe that You Already do…
I pray God grants Me This Blessing –
To Experience His Love to Me through You!

Now when God's Divine Love-Vessels
Share His Love to Them Instilled,
God's Love is then Extended
Through each Vessel His Love shall Fill.

And if We would Share with Others
God's Love Instilled in Me and You,
Then They too would Become His Vessels -
Sharing His Redemptive Love Anew!

Lord, grant that Your Love Divine,
Which Thou hast Instilled in WE,
Might be Shared with Countless Others,
That They Too Might Your Love-Vessels Be!

3/13/2020

The Game of Life

It matters not how the deck was cut,
Nor the rules that are set by Man,
Nor even the time the game is played -
Only how You play Your Hand.

When one learns the rules
And understands the cards that the table shows,
Then each player must review his hand,
And play the very best he knows.

Some plays may suggest You have no hope.
Other's plays may change your mind.
Then there comes that unsuspected play
That seems to suddenly catch You blind.

But the Game of Life is not always won
By the one whose chips are high.
Sometimes the one with the most to lose
Is the one who is next to die.

So play Your Hand with Wisdom.
And play Your Hand with Skill.
Whatever Cards Your Hand might hold,
Play them Each with Determined Will.

Know that Life's Game will soon be over,
And each Player must Understand -
What determines the Winners or the Losers,
Is how each one plays His Hand.

Remember also – each card upon the table
Was not designed, nor numbered, by those who play.
Instead, the Master of the Game of Life
Sets the Boundaries for every day.

So play Life's Game with Wisdom.
Study well the Master's Plan.
For when Your Hand shall have Ended,
Your Reward is in the Master's Hand!

2/10/2020

UNITY

UNDERSTANDING

*"Wisdom is the principal thing; therefore get wisdom:
and with all thy getting get understanding."*
                    - Proverbs 4:7

NURTURING

*"And, ye fathers, provoke not your children to wrath:
but bring them up in the nurture and admonition of
the Lord."*
                    – Ephesians 6:4

INTEGRITY

*"And the Lord said unto Satan, Hast thou considered
my servant Job, that there is none like him in the
earth, a perfect and an upright man, one that feareth
God, and escheweth evil? and still he holdeth fast his
integrity, although thou movedst me against him, to
destroy him without cause."*
                    - Job 2:3

TRUSTWORTHY

"He that is faithful in that which is least is faithful also in much: and he that is unjust in the least is unjust also in much."

- Luke 16:10

YOU

"For it is God which worketh in you both to will and to do of his good pleasure."

- Philippians 2:13

~

Samuel W. Hale, Jr.

Inside Deceit

⌒

"...the serpent beguiled me..."

That statement of confession revealed the reality of the subtility of **"deceit"**. In the early days after the Creation, one of the most tragic actions of the **"Woman"** – and the **"Man"** – resulted in what has been termed in the realm of Christendom as the "Fall of Man"!

A simple command – *"Touch not the fruit of the tree of knowledge of good and evil."* A subtle delusion – *"Thou shalt not surely die."* **"Do this, and experience what you were told you weren't entitled to." "Try that, and realize what you thought could never be."** The source of your apprehensions are often the cause of your limitations.

How is it that a creature that had once dwelled in the Presence of God, and had been cast from Heaven to Earth because of his rebellion against God, can lead a Soul created in the Image and after the likeness of God to disobey the Word of God? How does **"deceit"** find its way into the mind of one created to commune with God?

The answer lies in the reality of that word – **deceit! Deceit!** The Act of Twisting the Truth into a Lie, and a Lie into a semblance of Truth!

Deceit! The Process of Leading one to Believe a Lie and Doubt the Truth! **Deceit!** The Enactment of Wrong as a Substitute for Right! **Deceit!** The Falsehood of Believing that Disobedience brings Results that are Better than Obedience.

Enter the Serpent! The **Serpent!** A **Creature** of **Deceptive Power!** The **Serpent!** The **Living Essence** of a **Lie!** The **Serpent!** The **Pretender** of **Truthfulness!** The **Serpent!** The **Great Deceiver!** The **Serpent!** The **Adversary of God!**

It is the nature and ability of a serpent to move in a straight line from Point A to Point B – while moving crookedly! That's what **Deceit** is! A **Crooked move** from **Truth** to **Lie!** Whether crooked or coiled, the serpent deceives its victim into thinking it can outmaneuver the serpent. **Deceit unchecked** can be **deadly! Deceit revealed** ought to be **affirmed** – and also its **source!**

"...the serpent beguiled me..."

The Truth is that, sooner or later, Deceit will be Revealed. A Lie cannot live forever! And Deceit must be Confirmed. When Eve affirmed that declaration, both the Lie hidden in Deceit, and the Source of the Lie, and the Effects of that Lie, had come to the Light of Truth. The Consequences were yet to be affirmed, but that Lie could no longer prevail!

Beware! The "Serpent" still seeks to "beguile" You!

A Soliloquy On Deceit

⌒

To Lie, or to Live a Lie, That is the Question!
    Whether 'tis nobler to Commit an Indiscretion, and then Deny
    the Truth,
Or to Continue Living that Indiscretion, and ne'er Reveal its Truth?
    Alas, Nobility is lost in Both, and Credibility as well;
For soon the Truth must be Revealed, and Darkened Deeds must
come to Light,
    And, oh the Anguish and Dismay when Deceit is Put to Flight!

Consider now, my Friend, the Nature of Deceit.
    How once it spins its twisted Web, it Snares the most Elite.
How by design it Shades the Truth to make it Seem a Lie,
    While Indiscretions, kept in the Dark, are Hidden from the Eye.
How undetected it Plies its Trade and makes a Lie seem Real.
    But, oh the Anguish that it brings when no longer it can Conceal
The Truth that soon shall Come to Light;
    And, oh the Agonies soon Revealed when Deceit is Put to Flight!

Then should I now Admit the Deed that Tears My Soul apart?
    Or shall I Continue to Deceive, and Hide It in My Heart?
Shall I Pretend It ne'er Occurred, and Blame instead my Fellowman,
    Who in His Weakness might Succumb, or Fail to Show his Hand?

Shall I Decry the Deed He Did, and so vainly did Deny,
  While I, Myself, Chose to Hide the Truth, and Live – instead -
  a LIE!

And You, my Friend, where Standeth Thou when Lies Obscure the
Truth,
  When Deceit becomes the Rallying Cry from the Aged back
  through Youth?
Shall You Pretend that Lie You Praised shall Stand and never Fail,
  While the Scales of Justice shall Reveal the Truth that has been
  Assailed?
Shall You Decry the Truth Revealed, and Reality still Deny,
  While Looking into the Mirror at Yourself and can Only See
  a LIE!

Ah, Deceit, how Draweth nigh Your Ending Days when Truth before
You stands;
  How Strained Your Efforts to Prove the Lie that You Decry, that
  yet Expands!
It won't be Long before the Light of Truth shall Unveil Your Darkened
Ways!
  And soon the Blind shall clearly See, and the Deceived be soon
  Amazed!
For soon the Truth must be Revealed and Darkened Deeds must
Come to Light,
  And, oh the Anguish and Dismay when You - Deceit - are Put
  to Flight!

Samuel W. Hale, Jr.

1998

Expanded 2020

The Truth About a Lie

I greet you in the morning as your thoughts begin to form.
I nestle in your feelings – subtle - as if I'm the norm.
You may not sense my presence as morn to night goes by –
I have that **subtle** power – after all, I'm just a **Lie**.

I fill your mind throughout the day - even when the sun goes down.
In your sleep, I creep into your dreams, and never make a sound.
You may not sense my presence, but I'm always standing by -
I have that **hidden** power – for you see, I am a **Lie**.

Though I can be quite small, and my presence hard to find,
My preferred place of resting is in the shadows of your Mind.
You may not sense my presence, but I'm always standing by -
I have that **invasive** power – That's right! I am a **Lie**.

Once you accept my presence and make me feel at home,
I will give you the assurance that you are not alone –
There are others who are like you, some are far, and some are nigh –
I have that **uniting** power – after all, I am a **Lie**.

I can morph throughout your body 'til my thoughts become your own.
I am quite a fruitful gardener, once in you my seeds are sown.
Starting in your mind, I invade your ears, your hands, your feet, and eyes.
Depending upon your weaknesses, I can morph into many **Lies**.

I can spread myself beyond you, though you be my starting place.
I am not confined to your location, your persuasions, nor your race.
I can invade the minds of others as they may wander by.
I have **pervasive** powers – you see! I am an unfettered **Lie!**

I have clouded the minds of others who dared entertain my views;
And have caused more vacillations when Man's time is come to choose.
I've caused conflicts, wars, and tragedies, and countless Souls to die.
I have that **destructive** power – you see, I am a **Lie**.

I break up close-knit families, and cause nations to be at odds.
I like religious confrontations - pitting man's deities against man's gods.
I like defying moral values – even making Man think that he won't die.
I have that **devious** nature – after all, I am a **Lie**.

I invaded the Garden of Eden - I pitted God's Word against Man's Will.
My Luciferian powers in Man's Mind are active and effective still.
I cause Mankind to steal and murder. Some to gloat, and some to cry.
I have that **divisive** nature. Just watch me! I am a **Lie**.

I care not for God's Purposes, nor His Perfect Will for Man.
I care not for God's Forgiveness, nor His Eternal Salvation Plan.
I focus solely on my survival – that's the apple of my eye.
I plan to live now and forever – after all, I am a **Lie!**

I am known by many titles: misspeakings, falsehoods, and fibs,
Untruths, fake news, denials - and don't forget – retracted false adlibs.
It matters not what you may call me – though my words cause men to die.
My destiny is set forever – I will always be a **Lie!**

I like religion, sports, and politics - and gossip I can't avoid.
I influence science and human conflict – just ask Jung and Sigmund Freud.
My influence reaches deep down inside, and it causes Man to sin.
I'm a **Lie!** That's what I do. And I strive to make you my Friend.

I championed crooks and terrorists, politicians, and lawyers too.
Scammers, spies, and racists - even clergy! My influence they all knew.
I make the Wrong seem right. And the Right I make seem wrong.
I'm a **Lie!** A **Lie,** I tell you! My repertoire is strong.

Wait! What's that? The Truth, you say? No! No! The Truth I cannot face!
I'm a **Lie!** A **Lie**, I tell you! I'm not deserving of God's Grace.
When Time has run its limit, when God's Judgement Time draws nigh,
I am destined to Eternal Torment – I cannot change! I'll forever be a **Lie!**

Throughout Eternity must I languish with the Souls I have deceived.
Souls who then will regretfully wish the Truth they had believed.
Now that same Truth I must acknowledge - through Eternity without end.
Me – a **Lie** with the **Greatest Liar** - in Eternal Flames we both shall spend!

Just think! A Lie, conceived in Darkness, shall Eternally come to
   Light!
I must face the Godly Word of Truth that distinguishes Wrong and
   Right!
I must stand unveiled before Him! My Deceptions I cannot defend!
In God's Eye I am **still** a **Lie!** And the Truth of God won't bend!

Oh yes, I must confess to you, while it's fresh upon my mind -
Whether disguised, overt, or subtle, or even somewhat blind.
Remember, in whatever form that I appeared, or seemed I too have
   been -
At Your Mind's Door **I** was **still** a **LIE!** And **MY** Friend, **YOU** let
   me **IN!**

"…no lie is of the truth." – 1 John 2:21 (KJV)

**"Beliefs" Article printed in the State
Journal Register, Springfield, IL
Sunday, September 9, 2018**

BREAKING OF
THE CHAINS

Reflections on Emmitt Till

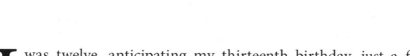

I was twelve, anticipating my thirteenth birthday, just a few months to come. Then came the word about another young teenager from my birth city Chicago. He was already fourteen, and though we had never met, something about him resignated with me. Summer was reaching its apex, and the excitement of visiting relatives also brought back many memories.

But! This time, disturbing thoughts and realities sobered my mind. My teenaged peer, Emmit Till, had been dragged from the home of his relatives by white men who were acting under the accusation that Emmitt had "disrespected" a white women by "whistling" at her in town.

The consequences were alarming! Emmitt had been kidnapped, beaten mercilessly, shot in the head, and left bound with barbed wire to a large metal fan tied to his neck, and thrown in the Tallahatchie River!

The heart wrenching pictures of that scene and the subsequent narratives of that ungodly event moved deeply in my spirit, and deep from within me evolved this simple lyrics with a haunting melody:

"Tallahatchie, Tallahatchie bound!
Tallahatchie, Tallahatchie bound!
Tallahatchie, Tallahatchie bound…"

It was that event that seemed to muster up my angst against the myriad racial events and experiences that I had heard and read about but had also personally experienced right in the local neighborhood, school, and local community in Decatur, Illinois. Realizing the reality that there were persons of like **"Money, Mississippi" mentalities** right there in my hometown, the challenge was heightened for **ME** to stand up against public, social, and governmental discrimination – still realizing that the **"Tallahatchie, Tallahatchie Bound"** Reality could also be **MY Consequences…**

Yes! The Days of "Emmitt Till" are Days of "Emmitt" STILL!

And **THAT Link** of the **"Ethnic Inequity Chain"** still is **Unbroken!**

The Homecoming Dance

───────────── ❧ ─────────────

While serving as President of our Junior Class, and a member of our high school Student Council, we had finalized the plans for our High School Homecoming Dance.

I was unable to attend due to my family being out of town attending a National Church Convention. Upon my return to school, I was immediately informed that one of the leading (white) Cheerleaders had been suspended from the Cheerleading Squad for dancing with one of the leading Black football players during the Homecoming Dance.

Realizing the then current Cultural and Ethnic Inequities operating within our city, and also realizing that THAT, and other Black football, basketball, and track stars, were the "glorified" reasons for our school's athletic prominence throughout the State, the purported reason for her "suspension" was still most inappropriate and unethical!

Ironically, no "restrictions" were applied to that Black football star with whom she publicly – under school supervision - "danced"!

Once again, my moralistic and "Equal Rights" inner nature led me to challenge the School Administration to address and rectify the Cheerleader Advisor's action.

Fortunately, THAT Link in the "Ethnic Inequity Chain" was Broken!

∽

"Whom Shall WE Send?

——————— ❧ ———————

Many times groups will convene and make decisions about what response may need to be made regarding some inequity that they might be experiencing. Such was the case for the NAACP organization during the 1961 Spring Semester at the University of Illinois.

The concern being addressed was the fact that many of the barbershops operating on and/or in the immediate vicinity of the campus did not serve the Black students. And the challenge was made! **Let's confront those campus area barbers!**

The die was cast! The Plan was approved. BUT! The Process needed a/some **"Guinee Pigs"**! Some "volunteers" to implement the Plan! So, **"Whom shall we send? And Who shall go for Us?"**

I could not speak for anyone else. But, already having been convicted of the need to **"confront the system"**, I volunteered to put my head and possibly my life on the line.

There I was, entering that specific barbershop, sitting down, and awaiting my turn. Rising above the staring eyes and frowned faces, I patiently waited.

Then the moment came! Next! I arose and went to the open chair. The barber looked menacingly at me and asked in a challenging tone, **"What do YOU want?"** Expressed or not in audible tones, the unarticulated inquiry included, in my mind, the question, **"What do YOU want...?"**

My unperturbed response was simply, **"A haircut, please, Sir."** With which the barber proceeded to do his job.

It didn't really matter that his "finished" results did not match any of my previous haircuts. BUT, the then current "system" had been confronted, and "change" had begun.

Ironically, my unexpected disappointment came from some my Black "civil rights" advocates. Their jeers of my new haircut were more discouraging than the disdained looks of those in that white barbershop!

Nevertheless, another **Link in the "Ethnic Inequity Chain" was Broken!**

On the Road to Selma

~

T he **March to Selma** was in the making! Thousands of people of many ethnic groups had arrived and congregated in the Black community of that Alabama town. The Civil Rights Movement was reaching a cataclysmic height.

In support of the Civil Rights Leaders to March to Selma, several Black students form the American Baptist College form Nashville, Tennessee, accompanied by one of their white professors, traveled in a two-car caravan to Selma, Alabama.

It was nearing dusk when we approached the city. Interestingly, as we neared the outskirts of the city, I noted that what appeared to be swampy areas on either side of the highway. At that moment, the memories of the many accounts of Black folk being drowned in such swampy areas began to fill my thoughts. Naturally, the lyrics of **Tallahatchie, Tallahatchie bound…"** came to mind!

Those soul searching thoughts were heightened when I noticed several pick-up trucks being driven by white eye and anger—glaring faces driving pass our "two-car" caravan. It didn't help to notice some of them holding their ham-radio microphones and speaking heaven-knows-what to heaven-knows-who else. Fortunately, we arrived unhindered on the Black side of town.

That evening, after having been assigned to the Family who sheltered us, we returned to the Church were the Movement Leaders led their Operations.

The next morning, after assembly, our group was assigned to "demonstrate" in a designated white community in Selma. While our group of Black American Baptist College students were demonstrating on one side of the street, another group of students from one of the prominent eastern women's university were demonstrating on the other side of the street.

Then, all of a sudden, several Selma Police cars screeched to a halt between us! Then, without explanation, we were ALL directed to get into the police cars!

And then, Irony manifested itself! At a period of time when a socially segregated period in time, when Black men and White Women were never to be seen nor congregating together, those Policemen, operating under "legal" authority ordered us to literally "override" the social and legal norms of the day. Both we Black men and those White women were "ordered" by those policemen to crowd into the "back seats" of those police cars! Forced Integration of Black men and White women in, of all places, the "back seats" of police cars!

Again, another **Link in the "Ethnic Inequity Chain" was Broken!**

The Integration of the Selma YMCA

~

I t is interesting that the **Young Men's Christian Organization** has from its inception stood for **"Evangelical Christian Principles and Values"**. Yet, like many **YMCA** programs throughout the **Nation**, those **"Christian values"** and **"programs"** were primarily available to the **"white"** members of the local communities. Thus **access** to the **YMCA programs** and **services** were **segregated – not available to minorities.** Such was the case with the **Selma YMCA** at the time of the **Civil Rights Movement!**

But Irony was at work again! That same day that those Black male American Baptist College students and those white female Eastern College Students were arrested and thrown into the back of those police cars in Selma, Alabama, Integration occurred once again.

Upon arrival of those police cars to the Selma Police Station, the concomitant arrests of others who had descended upon Selma had resulted in "filling up the jail"! Hundreds of other "arrestees" – men and women of numerous ethnic groups – were standing outside the overcrowded Selma Police Station!

Some may call it irony, others circumstance, but I call it Divine Retribution! God know how to turn a "stumbling block" into a "stepping stone"! Right behind, actually next door to, the **Selma Police Station** was the **Selma YMCA!** That afternoon and evening, overzealous racist persons and values incorporated "religious" resources which, in turn, accomplished a prophetic goal!

> *"And many nations shall pass by this city, and they shall say every man to his neighbour, Wherefore hath the Lord done thus unto this great city?"*
> *– Jeremiah 22:8*

That night hundreds of Souls from various nations, male and female, Gentile, Jew, Islamic, Christian, and of other religious persuasions were compelled, though by ungodly purposes, assembled together for a mutually moral and spiritually cause!

Resemblant in some ways of the Day of Pentecost, yet reflective also of that occasion when Paul had been arrested and thrown in prison in Philippi. During that evening, various Christian pastors, ministers, priests, and Believers joined with Jewish Rabbis and Jews, and some persons of Islamic persuasion, and also some persons of no religious conviction or commitment. Scriptures were read. Religious songs were sung. Prayers were uplifted. Faith-affirmations were shared. And God's Presence was Experienced and Felt!

Interestingly, resemblant of the verses in **Philippians 16:35-40**, the City Officials appealed to those of us assembled in that YMCA – become a "Church" facility! "Leave that Newly Integrated YMCA and return to the other side of town!"

While the Philippian passage cites that the Philippian City Officials' appeal occurred the **next morning**, the Selma Officials' appeal occurred **late** in the evening!

An old adage advises to **"Beware of Greeks bearing gifts."** That was such a moment! Those of us **"inside" that "jail"** were aware of the fact that the Klan and others who were angered by the influx of "outsiders" and "social interferers" of the Selma community lifestyle were unrestricted to express their animosities to those who promoted the **Civil Rights Movement! THEY** were **"outside"** the jail!

Thus the "response" to the Selma City Officials was that we would remain in that Selma YMCA "jail" until the morning, when we might be able to return more safely to the other side of town.

The events that later followed with the March to Montgomery and the expanded multitudes that assembled to hear Dr. King's prolific speech on the steps of the Capitol steps of Montgomery, Alabama were living affirmations that:

<blockquote>
Some more **Links in the "Ethnic-Inequity Chain" were being Broken!**
</blockquote>

∽

AFFIRMATIONS
- HALE-VERBS

A Wise Man Seeks the Counsel of the God who Directs his Life,
and a Trusting Relationship with the God who Sustains his Soul.

❧

God's Goal for Us is better to be Desired –
when compared to Ours –
than All the Ones We could ever set for Ourselves.

❧

The Man who is Not Sure about his Future
Is a Man who is Not Sure about his God.

The Man who Is Sure about his Future
Is a Man who Walks with his God.

❧

Who Best can Fathom the Mind of God
Than the Mind of the One who Regularly Communes with God?

❧

Be not surprised how God may speak to You.
If He can speak through a four-legged creature,
Surely He can even speak to and through a two-legged one.

❧

Wisdom is not "knowing everything"…
Wisdom is Exercising God's Perspective on What You Do Know.

❧

Sail not the Ship of Opportunity on the
Restless Seas of Regret and Shame.

❧

Yesterday's Deeds can Never be Undone -
Today's Decisions Transcend the Setting Sun!
Tomorrow's Race Must Still be Run…

Since Nothing Beats a Failure but a Try -
Then Try not to Fail.

There may be More than One Way to Skin a Cat,
but the First Step for Each Way is the Same -
Catch the Cat!

Don't Kill the Rooster because He didn't Lay any Eggs.

'Tis better to Swallow the Redeeming Tartness of the Bitter Truth
Than to Endure the Ever-Lingering Bitter
Taste of a Sweet Little Lie.

Absence may Make the Heart grow Fonder –
But, Unfocused, it may Allow the Mind to Wander.
And, if Provoked, it may Cause the Mind to Wonder.

Oh, the Overwhelming Power
Of Unexpected Joy!

It is Interesting how much We might Overlook the Obvious
While Focusing on the Expected
And Clinging to the Desired.

If Wisdom comes with Age,
Then seek the Wisdom of God -
The Ancient of Days!

Never let Anybody Else's Hang-ups Hang You up.
And don't let Your Own Hang-ups Hang You up.

What Has Been Done Cannot be Undone.
That Which Is Not Right Ought Never be Redone!

Affirm not what I may have Failed to Do,
So that Me You might Denigrate…
Affirm the Good that I Have Done…
And Appreciate!

I May be out my mind, but I Ain't no Fool!

It takes Two or More to Argue or Discuss,
But only One to Complain or to Fuss.

How Awkward it is to Fan the Fire that has Not Been Lit,
Or to Extinguish the Flames which No Longer Exist.

Time is just a Drop in Eternity's Bucket.

The Benefit of a "Long-Winded" Breeze
Depends on How One Sets Their Sails for Reception.

Be What You Is,
Don't be What You Ain't!
'Cause When You Is What You Ain't,
You Isn't!

(Compliments of Uncle Remus)

MAN AND WOMAN

Be Thou Not Alone

―――――――― ❧ ――――――――

Ine early morning in Eden's Paradise, God viewed the Soul that He had fashioned in His Own Image. The Creation Process had been completed with the Divine assessment - *"That it was Good"*! The Stars each traversed their assigned courses within their assigned galactical sections of the Universe. The Seasons began their assigned appearances. The Waters of the Earth performed their unending dance of silent evaporation, gentle condensation, and even tumultuous dispensation. The Flora punctuated the mountains, hillsides, valleys, and plains with their diverse differences and contrasting complementations. The Ichthusian Creatures paved personal pathways through the lakes and rivers and streams and seas. The Flying Creatures traversed the ethereal pathways with astute precision. The Creeping and Crawling Creatures settled and nestled into their respective routines. The Walking Creatures staked out their desired abodes. They all began their assigned routines upon the Earth – Two by Two. They were all Together.

But one Creature - God's Created Human Image of Himself – Man had no Complement for himself. Though He had been Fashioned out of the created substance of the Earth, and Endowed with the Divine Qualities of His Creator, and In-breathed with the Divine Spirit of His Creator, **something** was still **incomplete!**

Assigned to exercise "Dominion over the Created Order" in which he dwelled, there was yet no Complementation for himself. The Edenic Record does not reflect how soon after that Sabbath Day of Rest that God made one of the most revealing and affirming declarations for Time and Eternity. *"It is not good that the Man should be alone"!*

By Divine Decree or Natural Instinct, each of the other Creatures in the Garden with their mutual partners interacted with each other on their respective levels and in their respective roles on Earth. All except Man! Keep in mind that God's Role on Earth was not the same as Man's Role on Earth. Their relationships and interrelationships had their limitations. Something about **"Dominion"** is enhanced when two minds of the same nature are in harmony with each other.

There is something Divinely Unique when two independently created Minds of the same nature are in harmony with each other - while at the same time being in mutual harmony with their Creator. That reality puts a capstone on the concept of Divine Unity!

What an infinitely wise concept! Create a situation where the things created operate independently of each other, yet in harmony with the Will of its Creator and under the Dominion of its Caretaker, who operates in harmony with the Mind of that same Creator!

The die was cast! The systems were in operation. But, at that specific point in Time, there was only ONE Creature who had been so created to accomplish that unique task.

Only ONE Creature who had no like Complementation. Only ONE Creature who had no Complement with whom to interact on their own level. None of the other Creatures had been created like Man. So, no other Creature could act, nor interact with Man like Man. No other Creature had the same Divine Assignment as Man. No other Creature had the same Spiritually Divine Nature of Man, but Man. So, what better Reference Point, what better Resource for such a Compliment FOR Man than one like Man himself – yet with the Divinely Harmonious Qualities of the Creator?

With Man as the Model and the determined Will of God as the Guide, the very Supportive Portion of the Man – his Rib - was taken **from** him and fashioned **like** unto him. **Of** him, but **not** him. **From** him, but **of** herself. **Like** him, but also **like** unto her **Creator**. **Two separate Souls** with **one mutual purpose** – **complementing each other!** Helping each other fulfill their respective God-given purposes, to one Divine Conclusion – that the Qualities of God might be realized in and permeate the Created Order!

When a Soul is in harmony with the Will of God, then the consequences of that Soul's Work on Earth will bring Heavenly Joy to that Soul. When two mutually committed Souls are in harmony with the Will of God, then the consequences of those Souls' Work on Earth will bring Earthly Benefit, but also Heavenly Joy to both Souls. They share, not only the cooperative efforts, but they also share the Resultant Joy!

By himself, Man cannot experience the Joy of such Complementation! By himself, Man cannot experience the Joy of Complementary Results! There is something about being **alone** that stifles the **Spirit** of **Man**. Being **alone** prohibits the **"sharing nature"** of the **Soul** being fulfilled. There is also a great difference between being **alone** and being **"by oneself"**! Being **"by oneself"** involves a status of **position** or **location**. Being **"beside oneself"** is a state of **disorientation**. Being **"alone"** is a status of **relationship**. One can be in a crowd and still be or feel **"alone"**!

Aloneness affects the very essence of the **Soul**. **Aloneness** causes the **Soul** to long for interaction. **Aloneness** can cause the **Soul** to stray from its **Divine Purpose**. **Aloneness** can cause the **Soul** to over-focus upon **itself**. **Aloneness** affects the ability of the **Soul** to **monitor** itself, to **comfort** itself, to **complement** itself. Even to **love** itself!

"And the LORD God said,
It is not good that the Man should be alone;
I will make a help meet for him."
- Genesis 2:18 (KJV)

Every Soul Needs its Complement!

Every Soul Needs Another God-given Soul to Fulfill Itself!

To Become ALL that God Created It to Be and to Become!

So, to my Complementary Soul, I say -

Without You Near,
My Troubles seem much more to come.
I do not feel as One.
I have no Song to Sing.
I have no Hope for Spring.
My Heart feels Oh, so Empty.

Without You Near,
I Miss a Sense of Hope.
Your Voice to helps Me Cope.
That Something in My Heart
That seems so far apart.
My Soul feels Incomplete.

When Thou art Near,
All my Troubles Flee,
I'm no longer into Me.
I have a Song to Sing.
My Days Blossom much like Spring.
My Heart doth Overflow.

When Thou are Near,
Your Presence brings Me Hope.
Your Calm Voice helps Me Cope.
You Touch Me with Your Heart -
From Me, please never Part.
You Complement My Soul.

Samuel W. Hale, Jr.
Poem Written - 1967
Prose Written – June 1, 2018

God's Special Gift to Man

When God began to fashion
That Creature He called Man,
He used Eternal Wisdom –
God had a Special Plan.

God gave Man a special Body,
With uniquely performing Organs for many special needs
To maintain the tasks and functions
For Man's Body to succeed.

God gave him four extensions –
On two arms He formed two Hands.
On Two stable legs, He formed two Feet -
To accomplish what God had Planned.

On Man's Body, God placed a Head,
And inside, He placed a Brain
That surpasses the best computers,
For the work yet to be sustained.

A Brain to send and receive signals
From the Body's extended parts,
Guiding the functions of Man's Body -
When to stop, and when to start.

That Brain, while nestling in Man's Head,
Comprehends the World around,
And for that Body incorporates
The Laws that God laid down.

Also, inside that working Body,
God placed a working Heart,
To transfer special nutrients
For all the Body's working parts.

And inside that working Heart of Man -
Of special Qualities - with Godly Care -
God vesseled inside His Eternal Love,
For Man to Keep, and to also Share.

A Love that can control
All the Passions of the Soul.
A Love extending far beyond
Those things that soon grow old.

A Love that can and will forgive
All the offences of the past.
A Love - for all Eternity -
That sustains and shall forever last!

Conviction and Confusion

I know that I've been chosen.
I believe You have been too.
And I cannot shake the feeling that
God has something for Us to do.

I feel You close beside me,
Yet I feel some distance too;
And that distance begs assurance –
Is this a dream, or is it true?

With Tears I pray for Guidance.
In Faith I press onward as I feel led.
With great Caution I check my feelings -
I must not lose my head.

Lord, please Order my Direction,
And Keep Me from Myself.
Please Provide Your Divine Protection -
Without You, Lord, there is nothing else.

7/4/2018

My Prayer for You

May Your Body be Healed of its Infirmities.
May Your Mind be Freed of its Apprehensions.
May Your Heart Become a Sharing Vessel of God's Own Love.
May Your Spirit be Empowered by the Holy Spirit of God.
May Your Soul be United with its Divinely-fashioned Complement.
May You Become the You that God Created You to Become,
And to Forever Be!

4/1/2020

Hindered, But Not Halted

I know not why he broke your heart.
I don't need to know his name.
But I can sense the pain You feel,
Seemingly mixed with regret and shame.

There's something deep inside your Being
That seems somehow to have been destroyed.
Yet, God has a way to restore within You
The strength to fill that inner void.

What he took away was only part of You.
What he left was what he could not see.
Yet You still have left that Essence in You –
That Special Part that is Yet to Be!

Now he is gone, and You are left,
And Your Loving God has not left You.
There is much more of You to still Become,
When God's Plan You seek to Do.

Submit Yourself on Life's Potter's Wheel -
As marred clay from dusty sod.
And in the Potter's Hand You shall Become
A New Vessel that Pleases God!

Expectations and Limitations

I know not what all the Future holds
Between both Thee and Me.
But We can only be to One Another –
Be it Brother, Sister, Spouse, or Friend, or Lover –
As We both shall Let Each Other Be.

Your Place - And Mine

The Place of my Dear Departed Wife
Could ne'er Be Yours to take.
God's Purposes for the both of You
Twas for Him alone to make.

Now She is gone and You are here,
And Time moves on in constant beat.
God's Purposes now for You and Me -
We Both must strive to Seek.

For Me, I know not fully what He has in store,
Nor whatever Life may bring each day.
But this I know – God is in Full Control -
And in His Hands, I plan to stay.

So, whatever Plans God has for You and Me,
We Both must submit most willingly.
Only then can Our Purposes – respectively –
Be fulfilled by Each - Now and Eternally!

Privileges and Appreciation

If God should Bless You with the Privilege
to Spend the Rest of Your Life with the Person of Your Choice,
Who would that Person Be,
and What are You willing to Do to Show
Your Appreciation to God for that Blessing?

Marriage Preferences

———————— ❧ ————————

Would You prefer to Marry the One whom You Love -
That One Who Does Not Love You?

Or...
Would You prefer to Marry the One whom You Don't Love
To Spite the One Who Doesn't Love You?

Or...
Would You prefer Not to Marry the One whom You Do Love,
And to Marry the One whom You Don't Love?

Or...
Would You prefer Not to Marry Anyone -
Because You are Afraid to Love?

Or...
Would You prefer Not to Marry Anyone -
Because You are Afraid of Being Loved?

Or...
Would You prefer to Not Marry Anyone -
And Satisfy Yourself by Denying Yourself
the Blessing to Love and Be Loved?

Or...
Would You prefer to Marry the One whom You Love -
The One Who Also Loves You –
So You Both Can then Share the Blessings
of Loving and Being Loved?

Restrictions and Convictions

Tho' Our thoughts and feelings may have Led to,
Still I must not Bed You 'til I have Wed You…
And I must not Wed You 'til God has Said To…

Christmas Blues

Merry Christmas, Baby!
These bills have all been paid.
I said, Merry Christmas, Baby!
These bills have all been paid.
I know you wanted a mink coat,
But this is all the money I made.

Well, I couldn't buy a camera,
And I couldn't buy a car.
And I couldn't buy you a diamond,
'Cause my paycheck won't go that far.

So, Merry Christmas, Baby!
These bills have all been paid.
I said, Merry Christmas, Baby!
These bills have all been paid.

Well, I went to see my banker,
And I tried to get a loan.
But when he asked for earnest money,
I had to hurry on back home.

So, Merry Christmas, Baby!
These bills have all been paid.
I said, Merry Christmas, Baby!
These bills have all been paid.

Well, my plastic money melted,
And my bank account was spent,
'Cause I had to pay the light bill
And put a deposit on last month's rent.

So, Merry Christmas, Baby!
These bills have all been paid.
I said, Merry Christmas, Baby!
I done spent up all the money I ma-a-a-ade!

A Leech's Proposition

Hey, Lady, don't you want to share with me
Your Social Security, your Pension, and your Car?
Your Medicare Advantage Insurance Plan,
And that Room behind your Downstairs Bar?

I'll praise you for how you keep your house -
How you keep it nice and clean.
I'll even wash the dishes -
I won't ever make a scene.

I'll cut your grass, and rake your yard.
I'll wax your car 'til it almost looks brand new.
And if you'll wash my clothes and iron my shirts,
I'll tend to your flowers too.

I'll always be there right beside you -
At the grocery, or the picture show.
Be it shopping, dining, or your doctor -
I'll take you where'er you need to go.

I'll do whatever you ask of me –
I'll never leave you in a lurch.
But please, whatever happens,
Just don't ask me to go to Church!

A LOOK AT LOVE

Love is...

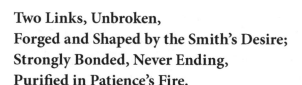

Two Links, Unbroken,
Forged and Shaped by the Smith's Desire;
Strongly Bonded, Never Ending,
Purified in Patience's Fire.

Love is...
 A Dove Descending:
 Gently splitting the Ethereal Sea:
 Proclaiming now the Heaven's Blessings –
 Completion of My Soul in Thee.

Love is...
 A Mountain Brooklet:
 Winding, flowing from the mountain's brink;
 Deep and cool and, ah, refreshing -
 Life is Death e'er I not drink!

Love is...
 An Evening Sunset:
 A Gift of color to the West;
 Golden, regal, yea, majestic;
 Crowning the day with peaceful rest.

Love is…

A Lamplit Window:
Beckoning, waiting for safe returns;
Lighting porch and yard and pathway;
It may glow faint, but for e'er it burns.

Love is…

A Morning Sunrise:
A Light that brightens every Day;
Fear doth flee – night shadows scamper -
And Life unveils a new display.

Love is…

A warm embrace:
In which Two Souls seem almost as One;
A silhouette against the moonlight;
A Spark to light the Morning Sun.

Love is…

A soft Caress:
A nibbling at a perfumed ear;
A Gentle Touch – most reassuring -
That bids Farewell to Doubt and Fear.

Love is…

A Tender Kiss:
Those warming, burning, inner fires;
A Conversation untranslated
In mortal words, but not desires.

Love is…
    Truth Uncovered:
    The Search that yields a Cherished Prize;
    A Yearning - nay, a Striving -
    The Heights to which the Soul doth rise.

        Samuel W. Hale, Jr.

True Love

Love Expressed when merely Spoken
Soon leaves One's Heart Deceived and Broken.

But Love that is Shared Before Birth through Sod
Is Love Infused with the Love of God.

Spiritual Dynamics of Love

⸻ ❧ ⸻

When two Souls allow the Love of God to Emanate and Permeate
their Bodies and their Minds,
then the Full-filling and Fill-Fulling of God's Love
will be their Mutual Experience!
For Both Souls shall then Experience
God Loving Them through Each Other.

❧

Love and the Soul

Liberates the Soul from Selfishness – John 15:12-13 (KJV)

Obligates the Soul to Reach Beyond Itself – Hebrews 12:1-2 (KJV)

Validates the Heights, and Depths, and Breath to Which the Soul Should Reach – Ephesians 3:17-19 (KJV)

Educates the Soul of Its Eternal Worth – 1 Corinthians 13:13 (KJV)

Samuel W. Hale, Jr.
August 30, 2011

My Love to You

My Love to You is a Gift
To Have, to Hold, to Cast Away
To Treasure, to Keep, or to Squander
My Love to You is a Gift

My Love to You is a Gift
Tender, Warm, Submissive
Disciplined, Guided, yet Intent
My Love to You is a Gift

My Love to You is a Gift
Surrendered, Yielded, Unrequested
Humbled, Opened, Emptied
My Love to You is a Gift

My Love to You is a Gift
From All of Me to All of You
Unlimited, Unsealed, Available
My Love to You is a Gift

- Samuel W. Hale, Jr.
May 25, 2018

Anticipation

I ring the bell, with the mental image
Of your smiling face in view…
Then at last, the closed door opens –
In that moment, with deep contentment,
I stand smiling back at You!

The Departure

The hardest thing, when in Your Presence -
When Time comes for my "adieu" -
Is to gaze upon your Visage,
And have to walk away from You.

Progression

When Your Mind is True
And Your Heart is Real,
Then the Love You Share,
No One can Steal.

And as You Share
Your Hopes, Your Fears,
Your Concerns for Each Other
Will be Endeared.

And soon a Peace
And Joy Sublime
You Both Shall Share -
In Spirit, Heart, and Mind.

And soon You'll Both Discover
That the Love You Share with Each Other
Is the Abiding Love for Both - You Two -
That God Shares Through the Both of You.

Invitations

You Invited Me to walk beside You
Along the pathway in the park.
You Invited Me to watch the sunset
As the twilight turned to dark.

You Invited Me to scan the Heavens
While constellations were on display;
Seems the hours were but minutes -
Soon the midnight turned to day.

You Invited Me into Your Dwelling,
And there inside, you sat me down
Close beside you, between two pillows -
There we listened to romantic sounds.

You Invited Me into Your Kitchen -
Eyes and nostrils did each fragrance fill.
A dining delight was spread before me -
All prepared with gourmand skill.

You Invited Me to Your Dining Table -
Ornately spread for two, with style.
Our conversation, enhanced with music,
By candlelight, we dined awhile.

You teased me outside Your Closed-door Bedroom -
With blinking eyes and moistened lips.
Then You hustled me to a flowered patio -
With separate straws, together, one drink we sipped.

You Invited Me in so many, many Ways -
Each Invitation was hard for me to part.
But, to me, Your most Cherished Invitation
Was when You Invited Me into Your Heart!

June 2018

Redeeming Love

How strong the Anguish of Untrue Love Revealed -
    The Pain that invades the Heart,
    That causes Hurt to be unsealed,
    And Angry Words impart.

How strong the Sorrow of Rejected Love -
    Expressed by one, but not returned.
    Undesired what could have been,
    By the other – Feelings Spurned.

How strong the Hurt of Love Rebuked -
    The Sadness that fills the Soul.
    The Incompleteness that is felt,
    The Void that soon unfolds.

How strong the Emptiness of Love Denied -
    What is, yet chooses not to be.
    While the Mind refuses to behold
    What the Heart can clearly see.

What Resolutions can then be found
     In situations of this kind?
     Where differences can be resolved
     Twixt Feelings, Heart, and Mind.

Ah, I believe, the Unifying Solution
     Resides where many Souls ne'er Trod.
     Except for those whose earnest Search for Love
     Yields them both unto the Redeeming Love of God.

Oh , Redeeming Love of God, draw nigh!
     Infuse Thyself in Me.
     Open my Mind to seek Your Will,
     So I will Yield my Heart to Thee!

Oh , Redeeming Love of God draw Nigh!
     Cause Us Both Thy Will to See.
     May the One whose Love Our Hearts Desire
     Be the Souls made One by Thee!

2/10/2020

The Greatest of These Is…

The Pleasures of the Flesh
And the Visions of the Mind
May wind their varied Journeys
Like the Extensions of a Vine.

But when Two Souls shall Know the Love
Of the Spiritual Heavenly Kind,
Know They then a Fuller, Joyful Bliss
For the Body and the Mind.

Know not You yet that We are Vessels
In which the Love of God can Dwell?
And that We can share that Godly Love
To many Others, just as well!

For when the Love of God Flows through
Those Vessels that It Controls,
Then the Love of God Empowers
Their Flesh, their Minds, their Souls.

And when their Flesh and their Minds become
Submissive Vessels of God's Own Love,
Then those Souls can Share and Experience
The Heights, the Depths, and the Essence of Love from up Above!

March 1, 2020

Agapeic Reciprocity

O, how Receptive might You Be
If God's Love to You
Was being Shared Through Me?

O, how Reassuring, if I then knew,
That God's Love to Me
Was being Shared Through You!

O, how then Fulfilling, when We Both shall See
God's Reciprocating Love
Complementing Both You and Me!

 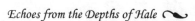

No Greater Love

If You would share the Love of God in You,
And I would share the Love of God in Me,
Then shall the Three of Us become
A Loving Trinity.

Since I Love God,
And God loves Me,
How awesome be the Love that's shared
When the Both of Us Love Thee.

I feel God's Love compelling Me
To Share Our Love with You.
For something about a Love that's Shared
Makes the One who's Loved Love Too.

I long to Feel God's Love in You
To Embrace and Indwell Me.
For then I'll Know God's Love in You
Is the Love that can Make Us We.

I know it is God's Spirit
That causes that Warming in my Heart,
When We are in each Other's Presence –
No more Alone. No more Apart.

It is God's Love within that Binds
Two Souls, who together Share
The Love that is of Kindred Minds -
Whose Hearts are Opened - Bare.

There is No Greater Love on Earth
Than that Shared by Two Souls and God.
Such Love Transcends both Space and Time,
And Brightens every Path they Trod.

There is No Greater Love on Earth
Than that Expressed by God's Darling Son.
And when We Share God's Redemptive Love,
His Love then Binds Us Both as One!

A Love That Lost Its Chance to Grow

It started in a Geometry class,
Where angles, lines, and circles on paper show;
In Chemistry Lab it continued -
Where the union of elements one soon must know.

Expanding over phone calls and school events –
Soon a friendship began to grow,
That was nurtured in spiritual values,
And personal convictions they treasured so.

From phone to phone, and face to face,
A deep relationship developed, slow.
Confiding to each other - hopes and interests still their own -
Their concerns for each other also began to grow.

Though they traveled different pathways,
Different subjects they chose to know;
From sophomore year through senior year,
Their Friendship did still flow.

Was it youthful immaturity
That caused that Inner Friendship Glow.
No, it was something else yet unrevealed
That they were yet to know.

Though they attended the same college,
Their personal futures sought they to know.
Their horizons began to broaden.
Their different directions began to show.

Then came that sobering moment when Her Dear Friend's Mother
    died.
Without personal consequences, her inner Care she did show –
She came to stand beside and comfort her dear Friend in his despair.
Beholding then her Presence, her Love for him he began to know.

Inviting him with comforting encouragement, in spite that
    moment sad.
Her Friendly and gentle conversation revealed a Love beyond a Glow.
It was that Special Moment that helped his Heart to understand
That Inner Love that translates what only the Heart could know.

That Inner Love that transcends the heights and depths of Life -
That doesn't resort to outward show for others to see and know.
But directs itself to the one for whom it cares,
With expressions deeper than the mouth and hands might show.

A new semester started, and that Friendship grew in kind.
That new Love now discovered brought its own special Inner Glow.
Quietly they experienced and expressed it, when those few chances
    came.
Reflecting and thinking, still they pondered what they had come to
    know.

Then came that fateful moment when the news was sadly told –
Her Family would be moving – to a new job must her Father go!
That semester's challenges heightened, and the future seemed unclear.
What now, O Love just blooming? When will again your Presence
    show?

The years went by in sequence - their Paths - slow and long to cross.
Mostly at Class Reunions, their smiling faces they did show,
Their Life situations, having changed – new careers did they pursue -
New Friends and Special Others came they soon to know.

Their own Families became their focus.
Of each other's Family – little did they know.
They persevered on their respective pathways,
Those decades could not extinguish their Friendship's Inner Glow.

The loss of Friends and Loved Ones,
And even Spouses, they both soon began to know.
When told, they consoled each other,
In ways True Friends and Lovers show.

They prayed, and called, and in earnest,
Their Inner Hearts did show,
That their Spirits had been connected
By a Power they both did know.

God's Love, that in them blossomed;
God's Love, in them was Known;
God's Love, that glowed and brightened;
God's Eternal Love, through them, was shown!

That Flame that in youthful hearts had kindled;
That Glow that in Us shown;
That Friendship that transcended decades;
Was just God's Love – We shared! We've grown!

That Love, though distance has made its impact,
That seemingly caused their Love to slow,
Though their Love was channeled to special others,
Yet through them still, God's Love they had to Show.

That Love – interrupted so long ago -
That Love that seemingly lost its Chance to Grow -
In their Old Age, understand they now,
It is God's Love that they still show.

I still Love You, My Dear Friend,
Distant though in Place and Time we've grown.
God's Love in Me transcends Life's boundaries -
His Love through Me to You must still be known.

I'll treasure the Hope You gave me.
I'll treasure the Care that You have shown.
I'll fan that Love Glow still within Me.
I'll treasure the Joy that We both have known,

Ah, Spark of Love that was lit in late September -
Three-score plus more quiet years ago,
That Spark - though only just an Ember -
Was A Love That Lost Its Chance to Grow.

Samuel W. Hale, Jr.
July 28, 2018

COMPLEMENTATION

An Independent Woman

An Independent Woman – unexpectedly -
Has come into my Life!
She has captured my affections -
Without coercion, and void of strife.

That Independent Woman
Has a Mind that's all her own.
She observes and thinks, decides and acts
Upon the facts before her shown.

That Independent Woman -
Her skills are known and vast.
She cleans and cooks, she sews and paints –
She even mows the grass!

She also works with people
Whose moral values seem not nigh.
Yet She strives to always emulate
Godly Values from on High.

That Independent Woman
Is known around the town.
She stands up with deep compassion
For those who've been cast down.

That Independent Woman
Does all she thinks she can.
But that Independent Woman
Has touched this Independent Man.

That Independent Woman
Knows not all that She has done.
For something confirms deep inside Me -
My Heart She now has Won.

What if that Independent Woman,
And this Independent Man,
Yielded Both to God's Transforming Will
In submission to His Own Plan?

O, Independent Woman!
This Challenge - May We Both Fulfill!
Let Us Both Yield Our Independence,
In Mutual Obedience, to God's Transforming Will!

Inner Conflict

How does one handle Inner Conflict
Twixt the Mind and twixt the Heart?
When the Mind says, "Journey Onward!"
And the Heart says, "Wait! Don't Part!"

When one's feelings for another
Begins to bud and blossom true,
And the Mind perceives a Future -
But the Heart avoids that view.

How does one person approach another -
While that Inner Conflict stands?
While the Mind is opened to Tomorrow,
But the Heart has other plans?

The Heart speaks her secret feelings...
She is slow to take a chance.
After all, who knows the Future –
Let alone, about romance?

There are things the Heart is seeking –
Things the Mind misunderstands.
Things that seem most important for
A Woman's Future with a Man.

Now the Mind, in deep reflection -
Views the facts seeming much in line.
But the Heart halts in disagreement,
For reasons seeming so sublime.

Oh Heart, what are you seeking?
What fuels your reluctant stance?
Why think your Mind's perceptions
Are simply based on happen-chance?

Are there hopes you see not possible?
Are there fears you must conceal?
Some expectations that seem conflicted?
Are there dreams you dare not reveal?

Oh Mind, what makes you so eager
To press your Heart to acquiesce?
Why do you think that your perceptions
For the Future are quite the best?

Aren't there things you've not envisioned?
Some realities you have not seen?
Consequences yet to be imagined?
Even fruits that can't be gleaned?

How can the Heart reach resolution
With a Mind so far apart?
How can the Soul find consolation with
Such dissonance twixt Mind and Heart?

O Mind and Heart together,
Please give this humble thought a nod –
Just submit Yourselves together
To the Heart and Mind of God!

And then - what e'er the differences -
You both shall still yet find
A yielded, humble Harmony
With God's Heart, and with God's Mind!

❧

August 2, 2018

How Near - How Far?

How does One measure Distance
Between Loved One, and of Friend?
What is the Rule of Closeness?
Can Separation ever find its End?

What is that Rule of Measure,
When Souls seem far apart?
I think I know the Answer –
It's the Warmth within One's Heart!

Be Ones Presence Real or Memory,
Whenever Spirits share – even be they miles apart -
Sparks of Love are soon rekindled
By the Warmth within One's Heart!

Samuel W. Hale, Jr.
December 25, 2018

What Shall I Be Unto Thee?

What shall I be unto Thee?
How shall You view We Two?
How-ever others see Us,
What shall I be unto Thee?

Shall I be Your Significant Other?
Shall I be Your Trusted Friend?
Shall I be just to You a Brother?
On what shall Our Relationship Depend?

How do You choose to view Me
As each precious Day goes by?
Who shall I be unto You?
How view Me within Your eye?

How I pray with deep intention
That You consider what You see -
Those strengths in Me – those things I lack…
Those things that You hope can be.

Am I the type of Man that You envision?
Am I potential "husband" bait?
Do I portray a Father image?
Is my age too young? Too late?

Does my income seem to You
Too small, or just enough?
Can We garner our Resources
For Days of Plenty? When Days are Tough?

How do You choose to view Me
As each precious Day goes by?
Who shall I be unto You?
How view Me within Your Eye?

While You ponder these Inquiries,
While You assess Your Future Goals,
Please include in Your Assessments
God's Purpose for Both Our Souls.

What is it that God wants for You?
What does God want for Me?
When God looks down upon Us,
What does God want for Us to see?

How I've pondered these inquiries.
How I've prayed for God's Will to Be.
I stand yielded to His Purpose,
And I pray the same for Thee.

Should I long to be Your Husband – Your Partner,
Your Provider, Your Protector – whate'er You need Me be?
Your Companion, Your Confidant, Your Complement!
All that can make the Two of Us be WE!

How I pray Your Understanding -
How I pray Your Mutual View.
How I pray to share Our Tomorrows,
Doing all God would have Us do!

Whatever I shall be unto Thee -
Down whatever Pathways We may have Trod -
However You may View We Two...
How Shall WE be Viewed by God?

True Relationships

When begins a True Relationship
Between a Woman and a Man?
What is the correct procedure?
Is there a standard plan?

When begins a True Relationship
Between a Woman and a Man?
Does it start with that first extended kiss?
Or when they publicly hold hands?

Does it start with frequent conversations -
By text, and especially voice?
Or does it wait to start its journey
When one makes another their special Choice?

What do you really call it
When their feelings are not in sync?
When one seems to be moving forward,
And the other has hit a kink?

When Tomorrow in one's thinking
Is prolonged in the other's mind?
Or the goals for one's Tomorrow
Are not clear, nor yet refined?

Is it not a True Relationship,
When they discuss their difference -
When they seek to describe their feelings?
Even when things get somewhat tense?

Is it not a True Relationship
When they share their inmost thoughts?
When they learn each other's feelings"?
When they declare their "musts"? Their "oughts"?

What shall I really call You,
When my Heart has been exposed?
When You know my inner feelings?
My thoughts, my cares, my woes?

What shall I really call You,
When my Love I did extend?
Are We not in a True Relationship -
Though You may view Me as just a Friend?

Ah, elusive True Relationship,
I think I've found you out!
Once two Souls have found Connection,
That's a True Relationship, without a doubt!

So, I declare with deep conviction –
Be you Lover, or be you Friend -
Since our Souls have found Connection,
We are in a True Relationship until our Lives shall end!

August 3, 2018

Why Me?

What is it that I have done to Thee
That turns your thoughts to Me?
What did I say that your ears still hear?
What did I do that holds your heart so near?

Was it the way that I held your hand
As we walked along the way?
Was it my hopes, my dreams, my plans
That I shared with you that day?

Was it the clothes that I chose to wear
On that evening that we met to dine?
Was it the way I held, with tender care,
Your shoulder close to mine?

What is it that I have done to Thee
That makes you call my name -
Whether I am near, or far away –
Why call Thee out to Me the same?

May I Come In?

I stand outside that Inner-You and Knock,
And pray You'll let Me In.
I sense Your Doubts, Your Fears, Your Hurts –
Those things You can't Suspend.

I stand outside that Inner-You and Call…
I know You hear my Voice…
Though the Pains of Present and of Past
May cause Conflict with Your Choice.

There is Room, I do believe,
Inside that Inner-You,
To Commune with a Soul that Cares for You,
And still allow to Yourself be True!

Please realize - You are Not Alone,
Even though You may Choose to Be.
The Spirit of Your God, with Mine,
Seeks to Comfort that Spirit Inside of Thee!

God's Spirit has been Inside of You
From the moment You were first Conceived.
It was quickened again Inside of You
When in Christ, Your Lord, You did Believe.

God's Spirit Speaks to Guide Your Thoughts,
My Spirit Seeks to Share Your Pain.
Together We are there - along with Yours -
To bring Wholeness to You Again.

Oh, how I Pray that Inner-You
Would Join with the Inner-WE,
To Release those Soul-constricting Bonds,
And Set Your Spirit Free!

6/29/19

Last Night and Tomorrow

Have you ever lain upon your bed at night and wished you were not
alone?
Have you lain awake 'til morning light, when the stars no longer
shone?

Have you thought of the one whose countenance fair you've often
gazed upon?
Have you wished that very one were there - with feelings like
your own?

What if that same someone revealed those thoughts that mimicked
yours?
What if those same thoughts were unsealed and shared through
verbal doors?

What might happen if those thoughts unveiled might reveal
unanswered prayers?
What if those same thoughts entailed some hopes, some fears, some
cares?

Oh, Morning Sun, your enlightening glow brings visions of another day.

When I arise, may I come to know that those same thoughts have come to stay!

May I seek that comforting hand to hold, of the one my thoughts reveal.

May the joys of days and nights unfold with mutual hopes, forever real.

10/26/18

Introspective Inquiries

~

My Soul Inquired of Almighty God how I might come to Know that Special One with whom We might Mutually and Complementarily Share the Rest of Our Lives Together.

The Answer that was Revealed to Me was simply this:

To that Soul whose Personage, Heart, and Spirit Reaches Out to You, Present this Introspective Inquiry:

> **"If it were Revealed to You that the Special Soul with Whom Your Soul might Mutually and Complementarily Share the Rest of Your Lives Together might Be ME, what Three Reasons might You give as to Why You Should NOT be Considered; and what Three Reasons might You give as to Why You SHOULD be Considered?"**
>
> **So, My Dear One, I Inquire of Thee, what might be YOUR Soul's Response?**

~

Your Visage

Your Visage is much more than the natural eye can see.
There exudes a natural beauty from deep inside of Thee.
There is an inner essence that only Godly spirits show
When free and uninhibited, and allow themselves to grow.

Your Visage speaks of heavenly thoughts and dreams
Which guide your human goals -
Yet denies those self-conflicting schemes
That betray so many Souls.

I've come to admire that Visage that bespeaks that Inner You.
That reveals a determined mindset of Godly Tasks to do.
I sense a directed Pathway that You follow with desire -
With a passion and commitment, like an ever-glowing fire,

And yet I sense a struggle, that within your Heart reveals
An unresolved connection, that still some resistance shows -
Seems a new direction - still yet a strong connection -
That Your Mind and Spirit knows.

As I gaze upon Your Visage - I perceive struggles deep inside.
Seems there are feelings, doubts, and longings - hard to quickly hide.
Be it Flesh against Your Spirit? Be it Mind against the Heart?
Be it Will against Submission? Be it a subtle Ending, or a brand new
    Start?

Ah! Your Visage demands attention from My Spirit - deep inside.
With prayers and meditations – and on God's Word You relied.
Determined, You seek Direction of a Future yet unrevealed -
"Dear Lord, please, Make Her come to Know Your Will - Unsealed!"

As I gaze upon Your Visage, I perceive an Soul so Fair.
I can see within – beyond Your Struggles - that God is standing there.
I can see an Humbled Spirit, Which Tomorrow soon will know
Down which Pathway You Must Follow - the Direction You Must Go.

Lord, please Bless that Humble Visage of the One whom I perceive -
That Soul that Thou art Guiding to a Future beyond Her View.
Whose Spirit Thou art Renewing, and whose Body Thou art Preparing.
For a Future and a Mission - with Another - They Both Must Do!

That Visage, with Grace and Beauty, does not control itself.
Whose Eternal Earthly Image is a Soul of God's Design.
Whose Earthly Purpose is God Determined.
Who daily seeks to follow the Directives of God's Mind.

My Love to You

My Love to You is a Gift
To Have, to Hold, to Cast Away
To Treasure, to Keep, or to Squander
My Love to You is a Gift

My Love to You is a Gift
Tender, Warm, Submissive
Disciplined, Guided, yet Intent
My Love to You is a Gift

My Love to You is a Gift
Surrendered, Yielded, Unrequested
Humbled, Opened, Emptied
My Love to You is a Gift

My Love to You is a Gift
From All of Me to All of You
Unlimited, Unsealed, Available
My Love to You is a Gift

- Samuel W. Hale, Jr.
May 25, 2018

Wishing and Longing

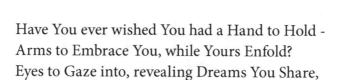

Have You ever wished You had a Hand to Hold -
Arms to Embrace You, while Yours Enfold?
Eyes to Gaze into, revealing Dreams You Share,
A Heart Embracing whom You dearly Care?

Where is that Soul who is My Complement -
Who is Herself, and Heaven Sent?
Whose Spirit Unites with Harmony
With the Spirit that belongs to Me.

Where is the One whose Mind Transcends
Those things on which most Souls Depend?
That One with whom I patiently long to Share
That Love instilled in Me with Godly Care.

Would That...

Would that Your Heart were drawn to Me,
As Mine has been drawn so long to Thee.

Would that Thy Spirit might also find
That My Spirit long has sought for Thine.

Would that our Minds be intertwined
Until We both Our Hearts shall bind.

Would that Our Hearts might share the Love
That comes only from Heav'n Above.

Would that God's Love – through our Hearts, in kind -
Flows from Mine to Yours, and Yours to Mine.

Would that Together We might fight Life's Fight,
And Together Stand for what is Right.

Would that when Life's Race for Us is Won,
Our Marks for Both shall be as One.

Would that when God's Face We Both shall See,
We'll Join as One – a Countless Multitude, God, You, and Me!

3/25/2020

Old Folk Still Can Fall in Love

Who knows better the Joys of Love,
Than those who have Truly Loved the Ones they've Known?
The Memories of their Yesterdays -
The Seeds they have Planted - the Blossoms that have Grown.

What makes an Old Man set his Gaze
Upon a Woman near his Years,
That Sparks a Flame within her Heart
That Dispels their "aloneness" Fears?

Why would a Woman of Extended Years
Open her Heart to Love's Refrain,
When Life's Experiences have Worn her Down,
And Joys, it seems of Former Days, have Trickled down the Drain?

Yet, Love's Moments too can Still Appear,
And Invade those Elders' Minds.
Who, once were Two, can again be One,
And through Love's Power their Hearts Entwine.

Old Folk Still Can Fall in Love!
For Age does not the Heart Control.
For Aloneness Fades when Love Appears –
And Refreshes again the Soul.

Oh Come, Sweet Love!
Invade my Heart. Embed your Pow'r Within.
Strengthen my Body. Renew my Mind.
Your transforming Pow'rs Extend.

Once I was Young, but now, I'm Old.
Health and Strength rubs swiftly Against the Grain.
But, when New Love Arrived, my Heart Revived -
Sweet Love has Returned, Again!

Ah, Love Returned, please Never Leave.
You've Filled Our Hearts Again!
In Our Old Age You are still the Rage.
In Us You shall Always Reign!

IN LIFE – IN DEATH

The Great Transition

The other day...
The Soul that once Complemented Me
Transitioned into Eternity.
I languish not, because I know
The Place to which Her Soul did go.

And yet I sense an Emptiness
Which Words alone cannot express.
I reach into my Inner Self
To understand what now is left.

That Soul, for years I grew to know.
Her Love for Me each day did grow.
We shared our Love, our Hopes, our Dreams.
We overcame the Tempter's Schemes.

We raised the Souls that through us came,
And helped them grow past hurt and shame.
We found new Friends and Loved Ones too.
Opposing Souls, we did eschew.

One day her health did take a turn
And caused my Heart inside to yearn.
We prayed. We sighed. We laughed. We cried.
And then that day - with Final Breath - She died.

I pondered while I watched Her go,
Why, in her pain, did She linger so?
What did She see, as She looked away?
His Face? His Hand? A Brighter Day?

Her eyes were set. Her face was calm.
Her breathing strained…Then She was gone.
What happened in that moment there
Was God's Fulfilment – an Answered Prayer.

We both had prayed, "God's Will be Done…"
We both believed in Christ, His Son.
Though Time had run its Scheduled Course,
We knew that Death must not be forced.

And then it came - Transition Time.
Her Soul embarked the Cloud Sublime.
No longer bound by Time and Space,
Her Soul Transitioned to a better Place.

I held her hand. I kissed her face.
Her then still frame I did embrace.
I wiped my tears. I sang a song.
Her Body lingered, but Her Soul was gone.

I wonder still what happens when
The Soul Transitions from this World of Sin.
But Assurance comes - Before the Sod,
The Believing Soul Goes Home to God!

❧

Reflections on the Death of Gloria M. Hale
Rev. Samuel W. Hale, Jr.
June 2, 2018

Transition of a Union

———————— ❧ ————————

Today, the eighteenth of August
Two thousand ten and eight,
I commemorate the Union Ending
Of my cherished wife of late.

In our fifty years of Marriage,
God blessed us with Souls of four –
And to our union entrusted He
A Gift of one Soul more.

Three Sons, one Daughter, and one Granddaughter –
Those Souls we sought to raise
And nurture with His Guidance,
His Mercy, Power, and His Grace.

We became part of each other's Families –
My People became Her own.
Her People received Me unto them –
One Family We had become.

Fifty years our Spirits mingled,
Harnessing Self, Desires, Impatience,
Ego, and Anger too -
Revenge and Hatred, we also did subdue.

In Him, our Souls did merge,
And learned in Him to Love.
We learned the Laws of Patience
And that Strength comes from Up Above.

We learned not to Live off others,
And not to live a Lie.
We sacrificed and bore our losses,
We shed our tears – then wiped them dry.

We endured much opposition -
Some even tried to break us up.
But God was watching o'er us,
And we sipped our Bitter Cup.

We shared in Kingdom Ministry,
At Home and on Mission Field;
We spread the Gospel Message –
God's Word - we did reveal.

We shared with other Cultures,
Many Ethnic paths We crossed.
Saving Souls was our Objective –
The Unsaved must not be lost.

Then one day, things began to change,
Two Souls, though knit as One,
Began to feel a Great Divide -
Her Race was almost done.

I watched the Cancer attack Her Frame,
And while Her Strength ebbed low,
I also saw Her Inner Strength
Increase with a steady Inner Glow.

I watched Her take Her Final Breaths.
It was Her Time - My Soul had Known:
She had Reached Her Destination -
That Day God Called Her Home.

There in Her Final Resting Place
We laid Her in the Sod;
I Yielded My Transitioned Marriage-Mate
Into the Hands of God!

Samuel W. Hale, Jr.
June 30, 2018

The Things She Left Behind

When my Wife of years now fifty departed to realms beyond,
I had to fathom in my mind what all had really happened -
In those years that seemed most sublime -
To ponder and consider what all she left behind.

She left behind some clothing – dresses, suits, and hats;
And shoes in different colors – heels and pumps and flats.
And jewelry for all occasions – necklaces, rings, and broches,
And things designed to hang suspended in her hair and from her
    ears.

She left behind some perfume and colognes with scents that still
    allure.
She left some fragranced lotions, and some soaps designed to cure.
I found small, shaped bottles of liquids in colors – only Heaven
    knows -
Designed to change the appearance of her fingers and her toes.

She left behind some pictures – some were taken long ago -
Of people I remembered, and others I still don't know.
Of some that brought back memories of places that we had been,
And things that we have treasured with our families, kids, and friends.

There were magazines, and pamphlets, and books with visions to
   extend
And stretch the minds and insights for those with time might spend -
Children, youth, and adults – new horizons might impart -
She even left some writings she had penned from her own heart.

She left behind some china, special dishes, and silverware -
From Family, Friends, and others – all entrusted to her care.
There was linen for the bedrooms. There were towels for body use.
Even non-descript containers – all kept without excuse!

There were also kitchen items – bowls and dishes, pans, and pots,
Appliances and gadgets – to keep things cold or hot.
Some in boxes, jars, and bottles, and some things that must be shook.
Some were liquid, and some were solid, even spices with which to
   cook,

Within each room she left behind some flowers and some plants,
Plant food and mulch and bug spray - for mice and ticks and ants;
Also, in the hallways, and the patio, and places in the yard;
Pots and buckets, forks and trowels, and things I must discard.

She left behind some items, for her own private use.
Some bring back special memories – some I'll keep without excuse!
But of all the things she left behind – from me will ne'er depart –
Is that Precious, Endearing, Godly Love still Exuding from her Heart!

MELODICA

I Need to Pray

I need to pray when I am sad -
When sorrows grip my Soul.
To ask the Lord, "Please cheer my Heart,
And make my Spirit whole."

I need to pray when I'm afraid –
When anxious moments come –
To ask the Lord, "Please light the way
That leads me safely home."

I need to pray when I am glad –
When joyful days unfold –
To thank the Lord for His Peace and Love
That satisfies my Soul.

O Gracious Lord, I love You so,
Because You died for me.
Lord, help me rise above this World,
And live my Life for Thee.

Samuel W. Hale, Jr.
1985

My Prayer

(To the tune "Oh, Danny Boy")

Almighty God Look down and Hear My Prayer today.
    Please Touch my Heart and Wash my Sins away.
Open my Eyes, O Lord, that I might ever See
    Glimpses of Truth that Thou hast Need of Me.

Then Guide My Feet along Life's Pathway Every Day.
    Lead through the Stones and Thorns along the Way.
Then Use My Tongue to Speak Thy Word to Every Man.
    And Let Thy Love Be Shown through Mine own Hand.

Forgive Me, Lord, for All the Sins that Stain My Heart:
    The Lust, the Greed, that Tears My Soul apart.
Purge out the Sins that Swell within My Selfish Pride,
    Make Me to Know, in Thee, I'm Purified.

Lord, Bear My Soul thru all the Flames of Patience's Fires.
    Transform My Mind to Seek What Thou Desire.
Redeem My Life that I might Live on One Accord
    With Fellowmen, and always with My Lord.

Bless then, O Lord, My Brother who in earnest tries
　　To Cause some Gleam to Fall within Mine Eyes.
And Let My Life a Faith Profession ever be,
　　Conquering Sin on Battlefields for Thee.

And when the Trumpet Calls My Weary Soul to Rest.
　　Grant then, O Lord, a Rank among the Blest.
Then Rock My Soul within the Cradle of Thy Love,
　　And Feed Me with the Manna from Above.

- Samuel W. Hale, Jr. © 1982

Sweet Baby Jesus

(Franz Shubert's Opus 52, #6)
"Ave' Maria"

Verse 1

Sweet Baby Jesus, Born in quiet Bethlehem.

The prophets had foretold Your Coming - You'd be Son oφ Man and
Son of God.

They traced Your Linage back to Adam. You are the Seed of Abraham.

They said Your Kingdom is forever – Where lions lay down among
the lambs.

Sweet Baby Jesus.

Verse 2

Sweet Baby Jesus, God sent You down from Heav'n above.

Your Mother was the Virgin Mary; And Joseph chose You as his son.

The Angels came and told the shepherds. The sky was bright like the
morning sun.

The shepherds left their flocks out on the hillside. They went to see
what God had done.

Sweet Baby Jesus.

Verse 3

Sweet Baby Jesus, Your Star shone bright in foreign lands.

The Wise Men came to You to worship - with frankincense, and gold, and myrrh.

They traveled home by another pathway, as God had directed them to go.

They shared the Word about Your Kingdom to Nations who had never known.

Jesus, King and Savior.

Verse 4

Lord Jesus Savior, Your Disciples spoke so much about You too.

They shared the words which You had taught them, Your Miracles, and Your Truth.

They told about Your Crucifixion – how You died for the sins of every Man.

They told about Your Resurrection – from the Dead, God had raised You as He had planned.

Jesus, our Redeemer.

Verse 5

Lord Jesus Savior, I came myself to want to know You.

You filled me with Your Holy Spirit, and taught me to live my Life in You.

I too believed the Gospel Message - I placed my Life into Your Hands.

I'm living, serving, watching, and waiting to be Raptured into Glory Land.

Lord Jesus Savior.

Samuel W. Hale, Jr.
© 2009

Give Your Life to Jesus

Are there moments when burdens oppress you?
Do the problems of Life press you sore?
Do you cry out when sorrows distress you?
Turn to Jesus, He'll open the Door.

(Refrain)
Won't you give now your whole Life to Jesus?
Won't you yield to His beckoning Call?
He will save you through this world's hard trials,
Keep your feet, lest you stumble and fall.

If ol' Satan should tempt you and try you.
If he sets his Hell-hounds on your trail.
Just remember that Jesus is able.
He can save you when all else will fail.

(Refrain)
Won't you give now your whole Life to Jesus?
Won't you yield to His beckoning Call?
He will save you through this world's hard trials,
Keep your feet, lest you stumble and fall.

I have trusted my whole to Jesus.
I surrendered to Him all my soul.
I'm determined to stay on my journey
'Til He comes to carry me home.

(Refrain)
Won't you give now your whole Life to Jesus?
Won't you yield to His beckoning Call?
He will save you through this world's hard trials,
Keep your feet, lest you stumble and fall.

Samuel W. Hale, Jr.
© 1982

Recorded by Albertina Walker - 1987

Because of Me

Because of Me, My Savior died -
On Calv'ry's Cross was Crucified.
The Price of Sin for Me was Paid -
By His Own Blood My Death was Stayed.

    Because of Me, Creation Cried -
    The Sun behind the Clouds did Hide.
    The Morning Stars in Sorrow Sang -
    The Earth replied in Solemn Strain.

Because of Me, in Joseph's Tomb,
My Lord was Laid to Change My Doom.
In Darkness all Alone He Stayed -
My Ransomed Price of Death was Paid.

Chorus #1
O Praise His Name, Who, Free from Guile,
Forgave My Sins - Made Me His Child.
Redeemed My Soul and Set Me free,
He Did It All Because of Me!

Because of Me - that Sunday Morn -
The Grave was Burst - Asunder Torn,
The Grip of Death was Paralyzed.
To Eternal Shores My Soul Shall Rise!

Because of Me, Christ Shall Return!
His Face Mine Eyes shall Soon Discern.
Through Cloven Skies He Shall descend
And Rapture Me and You, My Friend!

Because of Me, Dear Calv'ry's Lamb
Prepared a Feast - a Guest I Am.
With Saints, Who have thru Fires been Tried,
We'll All Sit Down - the Savior's Bride!

<u>Chorus #2</u>
Praise Him, My Soul, for I have Found
My Name is also Written Down
Inside His Book of Life, You See -
He Did It All Because of Me!

Samuel W. Hale, Jr.
©1985

Welcome Home

Oh, my Brother, O my (Sister), won't You please come Home?
Oh, my Brother, O my (Sister), won't You please come Home?
To that Land that's Oh, so fair -
I will meet You over there.
Oh, my Brother, O my (Sister), won't You please come Home?

Oh, my Brother, O my (Sister), won't You please come Home?
Oh, my Brother, O my (Sister), won't You please come Home?
The Lord is Waiting Over There
To Fulfil Your Longing Prayer.
Oh, my Brother, O my (Sister), won't You please come Home?

Oh, my Brother, O my (Sister), won't You please come Home?
Oh, my Brother, O my (Sister), won't You please come Home?
You have Run Your Race so long,
And Your Faith You have keep Strong.
Hear Christ say, Oh, My Brother, O my (Sister), Welcome Home!

Indices

Prose

<u>Poems</u>

Melodica

# # #

Printed in the United States
by Baker & Taylor Publisher Services